# NUT:
## ANCIENT EGYPTIAN COSMIC MOTHER OF ETERNITY

# NUT:
## ANCIENT EGYPTIAN COSMIC MOTHER OF ETERNITY

MERITKA

# NUT: ANCIENT EGYPTIAN COSMIC MOTHER OF ETERNITY

iUniverse books may be ordered through booksellers or by contacting:

iUniverse
1663 Liberty Drive
Bloomington, IN 47403
www.iuniverse.com
844-349-9409

Because of the dynamic nature of the Internet, any web addresses or
links contained in this book may have changed since publication and
may no longer be valid. The views expressed in this work are solely those
of the author and do not necessarily reflect the views of the publisher,
and the publisher hereby disclaims any responsibility for them.

Any people depicted in stock imagery provided by Getty Images are
models, and such images are being used for illustrative purposes only.
Certain stock imagery © Getty Images.

ISBN: 978-1-6632-4491-8 (sc)
ISBN: 978-1-6632-4492-5 (e)

Library of Congress Control Number: 2022916210

Print information available on the last page.

iUniverse rev. date: 09/08/2022

To my mother, Mary, who inspired my
search for the divine feminine, the divine
mother, and the heavens; Nut.

Words spoken by the Osiris, the royal scribe Amenhotep:
"O my mother Nut, stretch yourself over me that
I may be placed among the imperishable stars
which are in you and that I may not die."
—Erik Hornung and Betsy M. Bryan

# Contents

Preface.................................................................xi

Introduction......................................................xiii

Nut and the Spiritual Rebirth of the King........................ 1

Hymn to Nut.................................................... 11

Nut: Tree Deity ................................................ 23

Conclusion...................................................... 31

Glossary ....................................................... 33

References ...................................................... 35

About the Author............................................... 37

# Preface

Mother deities were important in ancient societies. In ancient Egypt, the great mother deity, Nut, was not an earthly goddess but a heavenly one. In ancient Egyptian cosmogony, Nut was the preeminent sky goddess, who gave birth to the sun, moon, and stars daily through her cosmic womb. The sky was conceptualized as a mother who gives birth to the cosmos.

In ancient Egyptian eschatology, scribes and priests were the purveyors of the belief in the immortality of the soul. At the time of his death, the soul of the king would reign in the sky with his father, the sun god Ra. An Egyptian king was reborn into an eternal life through ancient rituals and ceremonies that would cause him to travel through the womb of his eternal mother, Nut (the sky). As a son of Ra, the deceased king was conceived in the womb of Nut and spiritually reborn as a shining eternal spirit (*Akhw*).

As the Egyptians evolved in their spiritual ideas, Nut became the mother of not only deceased kings but anyone transitioning from mortal death to immortality. An image of her as the sky with stars over her body was carved on the ceilings of the tombs of these ancient kings. The stars painted on the ceilings represented the heavens the deceased king would travel to, and these heavens were the sky goddess's body. During the Middle Kingdom (2100–1500 BCE), the sky deity's image was painted on the coffins of the dead. Conceptually, each person born into the mortal world through their mother's womb was then reborn into everlasting life through the cosmic womb of Nut. This book seeks to explore the relationship between the divine mother, Nut, and her role in the kings of Egypt's spiritual rebirth.

# Introduction

In ancient Egypt, Nut, the sky deity, was integral in the cosmogony and eschatology surrounding the soul's journey to eternity. The cycle of the sun was a metaphor for the king's path to eternal life. Resembling his father, Ra, the sun deity, the king's spirit traveled through Nut's body (the sky) to daily rebirth.

Nut (the sky) enclosed the earth. She also enclosed the king's coffin since her image was drawn on the ceiling of the ancient tombs. The king's mummified body was enclosed in the coffin, then the coffin was enclosed in the tomb. The images of Nut on the tomb's ceiling depicted the journey to the afterlife through the sky.

Nut was one of the nine deities named in the creation story of the sun god's ancient city, Iunu (Heliopolis). As an aspect of this creative principle, the mother deity provided the deceased king with passage through the darkness of the heavens (her womb). As the cosmic womb, Nut was the waterway the king traveled through to reach eternity after death. This book will explore the relationship Nut had with the Old Kingdom's king's death and transition to eternal life in ancient Egypt.

Nut guided, nurtured, protected, and birthed the deceased king to a renewed life as an Akh or eternal spirit. Written on the walls of the king's tomb were hieroglyphic texts of the rituals that assisted the king in his transformation to an Akh. These texts were known as the Pyramid Texts and document the great mother goddess's role in the king's transformation.

In the royal mortuary liturgy, the king traveled the night sky through the cosmic womb of Nut. Led by Nut and Ra, he was reborn with his father on the eastern horizon to reign in the heavens as an astral being (Akh) each day. In the tombs of the kings, the priests would recite the rituals that would restore the king's body and transform him in anticipation of his journey through the night sky.

The rituals recited by the priests at the time of the king's death would implore the king's spiritual parents to transform him into an eternal spiritual being. The divine mother protected the king's spirit as it traveled to and through the heavens to immortality.

# Nut and the Spiritual Rebirth of the King

The first creation story of Egypt originated in Iunu. Ancient Egyptians conceptualized creation as the result of the natural phenomena of the cosmos. The unique aspects of creation were told as a story depicting a "family" of deities in the cosmogony. This family of deities were integral in the origin of the world. Each deity was a personification of an aspect of nature. The analogy of a family of deities appears throughout the creation myths. The creator had daughters, sons, granddaughters, grandsons, and humans as their progeny. Motherhood was sacred in Egypt and depicted in royal iconography, myths, rituals, and temple reliefs. Images of the female/mother principle as snakes/cobras, vultures, trees, water, cows, lionesses, and birds were all used to symbolize motherhood. Hathor was a cow goddess; Mut's symbol was the vulture; Wadjet's was the cobra; Sekhmet's was the lioness; and Nut was the watery sky. Nut was one of the great mothers and a deity of the divine nine (Ennead) cosmogony of Iunu.

In the cosmogony, life began when the sun, Atum-Ra, was born and arose from the primordial waters, just as humans come alive when they are born from the waters of their mother's womb. The sun—the creative principle that illuminated the earth—was born of the cosmic ocean of the heavenly womb each morning. In the rooftop chapel of the Temple of Hathor at Dendera, Egypt, there is an image of the daily transit of the sun through Nut's body (the sky). This image depicts Nut with stars over her body, arched over the earth, just like the heavens, and the sun traveling through her before being reborn through her womb at sunrise, and then shining on an image of Hathor, his daughter. This image depicts the ancient Egyptians' view of the sky as the divine mother that swallowed the sun at night and gave birth to it each morning.

The daily "rebirth" of the morning sun was thought to represent a birth from the cosmic mother. "As for Nut, the heavens, here identification in the iconography and in most texts such as the *Book of Hours* is with the mother, i.e. the one who gives birth to the sun … and who bore the gods" (Carruthers, 34). In the *Book of the Dead*, spell 24 states, "I am Atum-Khepri who came into being of himself upon the lap of his mother Nut" (Faulkner 2005, 55). Atum-Khepri, the rising morning sun, was born of the cosmic mother and reborn daily. In a "Hymn to the Sun God," it states, "Khepri of distinguished birth, who raises his beauty in the body of Nut" (Lichtheim 2006, 88). Nut was central to the rebirth and renewal of the sun. In her role as the sky goddess, she was the repository of time as reflected in the cycles of the sun, moon, and stars to which she gave birth.

In ancient societies, the female was the marker of time and gave life to humanity. Priests utilized natural phenomenon to describe the heavens as a cosmic womb that gave birth to heavenly bodies. It is an idea the human mind conceptualized for the mythology of creation. The concept of the cosmic mother giving birth to life was visualized as the same process of a natural human birth. "The sun's disappearance ('inside' the sky) at night and its reappearance each morning suggested to the Egyptians a cycle of death and rebirth. This in turn pointed to the feminine character of the sky, conceptualized in the goddess Nut, 'who gives birth to the Sun every day' (Pyr. 1688b). Her name (Nut) may be a feminine adjective meaning 'of the waters,' though the etymology is far from certain" (Allen, 5).

In the ancient Egyptian creation myth, Geb (the earth) and Nut gave birth to Osiris/Wosir, Seth/Setekh, Isis/Aset, and Nephthys/Nebethet. Her children became integrally involved in the story of divine kingship. Osiris, Nut's eldest son, was considered the first Egyptian king. At the time of his death, and later resurrection, he became the king of the dead, or ancestors who lived in the west. In Egyptian eschatology, Nut became the mother of all deceased kings because they embraced the persona of Osiris in the rituals for resurrection found in the Pyramid Texts. As the figurative mother of the deceased king she was the womb (i.e., the coffin or sarcophagus) that enclosed his mummy in the tomb, and the sacred mother that enclosed him in the dark of the heavens (*Duat*). In the dark of the heavens, she transforms the king's spirit into an Akh. Nut spiritually bore the deceased king just as she did the sun every day. From this birth, the king ascended as an astral body to his father, Ra, who was also a star in the heavens. The king, who was divine, incorporated the cycle of the sun as an astral being. There were three divinized cycles of the sun's transit through the sky: Khepera, the rising sun; Ra, the noonday sun; and Atum, the setting sun.

> But it is accepted that parts of the Pyramid Texts reflect the burial of the king, his existence in the tomb, and his participation in the daily journey of the sun. At sunset, according to these texts, the "old" king enters his crypt as the god Ra-Atum, a manifestation of the evening sun. The king spends the night in the tomb, which represents the netherworld, and is there united with Osiris, in the form of the king's own mummy. Recently, I.E.S. Edwards has theorized that the royal stone sarcophagus was thought of as the body of the sky goddess Nut, the mother of Osiris, a concept Edwards traces back to Khufu, the first king buried in a stone sarcophagus. At sunrise, the king is reborn and leaves his sarcophagus as the young god Khepri. The god king departs from his resting place through the antechamber of the crypt and starts a new cycle of life, ascending to the sun as the mature sun god Ra-Harakhti. (Shafer, 71)

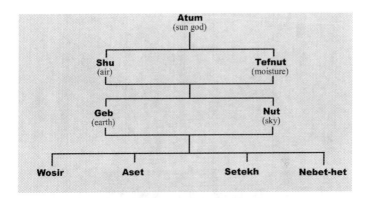

Canstock photo
Osiris with the white crown (Hedjet) of Ancient Egypt.

Canstock photo
Isis wearing a throne headdress.

Seth
En.wikipedia/Seth

Nephthys
En.wikipedia.com/nephtys

Canstock photo
Pyramid texts in King Unas tomb, fifth dynasty.

"The Pyramid Texts were funerary inscriptions that were written on the walls of the early ancient Egyptian pyramids at Sakkara. These date back to the fifth and sixth dynasties, the years 2350–2175 B.C.E. However, because of extensive internal evidence, it is believed that they were composed much earlier, circa 3000 B.C.E. The Pyramid Texts are, therefore, the oldest sacred texts known" (Mercer 2008). The Pyramid Texts were the royal rituals and recitations for the king's journey to eternity and divinity. Mortuary priests would recite the rituals for spiritual transformation over the deceased king's body. Other deities helped the king in his journey to the afterlife, however, Ra and Nut were his only spiritual father and mother.

> Homage to you, Ra, you who travels across
> the sky and heavens, having traversed the
> Winding Waterway. I have grabbed hold of

> you for myself, for I am a god and the sun
> of God. (Karenga 1984, 123–124)

The waters, or "winding waterway," are the path through the lower sky, or womb, of the cosmic mother. Symbolically, the sky was a cosmic ocean that the sun sailed in his barque (boat) every night. Mythically, the deceased king makes this same journey. In ancient Egypt, the west was considered the realm of the dead because the sun set (or "died") in the western horizon. Nut protected the king on his journey from the forces of darkness. The Pyramid Texts state, "O King, your mother Nut has borne you in the west; go down to the west as a possessor of honor" (Mercer 2008, 403). These texts describe how the king was given his divinity by Nut during his transition to eternal life. "… O Nut set your hand on me with life and dominion, that you may assemble my bones and collect my members. May you gather my bones at (?) … there is no limb of mine devoid of God. May I ascend and lift myself up to the sky as the great star in the midst of the East." (Faulkner, 173). The king, in this recitation from the texts, asked the divine mother to spiritually restore the bones of his body and allow him to ascend to the sky as the sun.

At his time of death, the king took on the identity of Osiris, and his spiritual birth was conceived between Ra and Nut. "Ra, impregnate the body of Nut with the seed of the spirit which shall be in her" (Mercer 2008, 258). These words, recited by priests, caused Ra to metaphorically plant his spiritual seed in Nut's womb, and he was reborn from her womb a divine being—as the mythical King Osiris.

In the Pyramid Texts, there are a series of recitations to Nut known as the "Hymn to Nut," or "In Praise of Nut." This hymn describes Nut's role as divine mother and the one who creates the king in her womb for rebirth. In the hymn, she forms King Pepi in her womb so that he may be spiritually reborn in the sky. King Pepi refers to himself as Osiris, Nut's son. He was transformed into an eternal spirit in the sky, and he is one of her children. King Pepi does not die; he becomes divine. In the hymn, King Pepi asks his mother, Nut, if he may stay in her (the cosmic womb) like an imperishable star—an astral body—since she gave birth to the stars. He requests to become eternal. To become eternal, King Pepi must be fashioned (formed) into an astral being in the sky. "Originally a personification of the sky, Nut became a funerary goddess in the sense that the deceased person would expect to be wrapped in her body and become part of the heavenly host and "transformed in his journey to the duat where he becomes an Akhw, eternal spirit" (Carruthers,68).

Canstock Photo

Nut, with her name in hieroglyphs above her.

(The pot means "Nu" and half loaf means "t" with the sky determinative.)

# Hymn to Nut

O *Nut*, spread yourself over your son the Osiris (Pepi),

That you may conceal him from Set; protect him, *Nut*.

Have you come that you may conceal your son?

I have indeed come that I may protect this great one. Osiris Pepi.

O *Nut*, fall over your son the King, protect him.

O Great Protectress (even) this great one who is among your children.

Thus, says Geb, O *Nut* it is well with you; power was yours in the womb

of your mother Tefnut before you were born, that you might protect this King,

for he has not died.

You are strong in your mother's womb in your name of *Nu*t.

You are the daughter, mighty in her mother,
who appeared as a bee
make the King a spirit within yourself, for
he has not died.
You did leap in the womb of your mother
in your name of "*Nut*."
O Great Lady, one who did come into being
in the sky, you have achieved power.
Who does make happy, and you have filled
every place with your beauty,
The entire earth is under you, take
possession of it.
You have enclosed the earth, and all things
within your embrace,
You have set this King (Pepi) as an
imperishable star who is in you.
I have made you fruitful (?) by means of
Geb in your name of Sky.
For I have joined the entire land to you
everywhere.
O mistress over the earth, you are above
your father Shu, you have the mastery
over him.
He has loved you so much that he set
himself under you in all things.
You have taken to yourself every god who
possesses his bark.
That you may install them in the starry sky.
Lest they depart from you as stars.

Do not let this King (Pepi) be far from you
in your name of sky.
(Faulkner, 141)

"The Hymn to Nut" reflects the fundamental views regarding the king's spirit. His soul was astral, like his spiritual father's. Osiris, as Nut's son and the deceased king, was king of the dead in the land of the dead (Amenta).

The hymn describes Nut's conception, birth, and origins in the sky. Her titles included "Great Lady" and "Mistress over the Earth." She installed the gods in the starry sky, and allowed for King Pepi to become an imperishable star by installing him in the night sky as well. If he was reborn as a star in the sky, he would then become immortal. Only Nut has the power to set King Pepi as an imperishable star in her (the sky). Nut had mastery over her father, Shu, because the heavens control the wind (air). As the sky enclosed the earth, Nut enclosed the king.

In the below quote, Nut is speaking of her son, Osiris, whom the deceased king transitioned into.

> Recitation (words spoken) by Nut the great who dwells in the Mansion of Snit (A shrine of On -Iunu-city of the sun). The King is my son of my desire; I have given to him the Netherworld (Duat) that he may preside over it as Horus who presides over the Netherworld (Duat). All the gods say: Your father Shu knows that you love the King more than your mother Tefnet. (Mercer 2008, 25)

> Recitation (words spoken) by Nut: I enfold your beauty within this soul of mine for all life, permanence, dominion, and health for the King—may he live forever! (The "soul" of Nut here is the coffin bearing her name which encloses the body of the king.) (Mercer 2008, 26)

Nut was the nurturer and protector of the dead. The deceased appealed to her as a child appeals to its mother. "O my Mother Nut, stretch Yourself over me, that I may be placed among the imperishable stars which are in You, and that I may not die." Nut was thought to refresh the dead with food and wine once they were in her (sky). "I am Nut, and I have come so that I may enfold and protect you from all things evil." The divine mother began the funerary ritual in the Pyramid Texts with her love for her son, Osiris. The first utterance of the Pyramid Texts states, "The Heavens declare this royal vindicated one is my beloved son in whom I am well pleased … my first born upon the throne of earth" (Karenga 1984, 119). The Pyramid Texts found in King Unas's tomb describes how he prayed to Nut for ascension.

> The King ascends to the sky
> This Unas comes to you, O Nut,
> This Unas comes to you O Nut,
> He has consigned his father to the earth,
> He has left Horus behind him.
> Grown are his falcon wings,
> Plumes of the holy hawk.
> His power has brought him,

His magic has equipped him!
The Sky-goddess replies
Make your seat in heaven,
Among the stars of heaven,
For you are the Lone Star, the comrade of Hu!
You shall look down on Osiris,
As he commands the spirits,
While you stand far from him.
You are not among them,
You shall not be among them!
The King prays to the sky-goddess
O great strider
Who sows greenstone, malachite,
turquoise-stars!
As you are green so may Teti be green,
Green as a living reed!
(Lichtheim 1975, 32–33)

"I have come to you O Mother of Heaven. I have duly buried my father and left Horus, the new Pharoah behind me … my words of power have made me effective" (Karenga 1984, 125). The Akh was an effective one. The effective one referred to a shining being that had transitioned from death to eternal life. As the king transitions to eternity, he states that he completed his earthly duties, was a good son, he buried his father, and left his kingdom to his son, Horus. As a comrade of Hu, the king retains his royal authority in the afterlife. He will not be in the realm of the dead, but instead, will be reborn and live forever. Nut commands the king and recites the divine words for his transformation. She purified and cleansed him for initiation into eternity. She implored him to awake (resurrect) and stand up. Restored and resurrected, his children no longer mourn him because he is "alive" forever.

> Nut comes to you, so you will not lack; the Great Protectress comes to you so you will not lack; the Protectress of the frightened, so you will not lack. She will protect you, she will prevent you from lacking, she will give you your head, she will reassemble your bones for you, she will join together your members for you, she will bring your heart into your body for you, that you may be at the head of those who are at your feet, that you may give orders to those who are in your presence, that you may perpetuate your house after you, and that you may prevent your children from mourning. Your purity is the purity of the gods, the Lords of affairs who have gone to their doubles.

> O King, awake! Raise yourself! Stand up, that you may be pure and that your double may be pure, that your soul may be pure, that your power may be pure. Your mother comes to you, Nut comes to you, the Great Protectress comes to you that she may cleanse you, O King; that she may protect you, O King and that she may prevent you from lacking.

Be pure! Your mother Nut, the Great Protectress purifies you, she protects you! (Faulkner, 150)

O King, your mother Nut spreads herself over you that she may conceal you from all evil, for she has protected you from all things evil, and you are the greatest of her children. (Faulkner, 148)

Photo by Author
An image of Nut and Ra, with the sun transitioning her body, on the ceiling above the tomb of Ramesses IV.

Nut's divine words or utterances birthed the king into an astral body. Spiritually, the heavens were the realm of existence in which he traveled through the night sky. He emerged from the dark of her womb reborn on the eastern horizon and transformed into an Akh. The motif for the sun's journey to rebirth was the metaphor for the king as his son.

> Receive your natron that you may be
> divine, for Nut has caused you to be a god
> to your foe in your name of God. (Mercer
> 2008, 210)

"O Nut spread yourself over your son Osiris the King that you may conceal him from Seth, protect him O Nut" (Faulkner, 141). Nut welcomed him to heaven, and he became a star. "O Great One who became Sky, you are strong, you are mighty, you fill every place with your beauty. The whole earth is beneath you, you possess it! As you enfold earth and all things in your arms, so have you taken this Pepi to, an indestructible star within you!" (Lichtheim, 44). The prayers addressed to Nut ask her to take the deceased king into her arms and transform him into a star.

> Ascend to your mother Nut; she will take
> your hand and give you a road to the horizon,
> to the place where Ra is. (Faulkner, 139)

> O Nut, if you live, then the King will live.
> (Faulkner, 148)

The king became the successor of Osiris and was crowned for eternity. Utterance 422 of the texts was titled, "The King becomes a spirit." The "words of power," as mentioned earlier, began his ascension into the sky.

> O King, go that you may be a spirit and
> have power as a god, as the successor of
> Osiris; you have your soul within you,
> you have your power about you, you have

your Wrrt-crown upon you, you have your
Mizwt-crown upon your shoulder. …
Ascend to your mother Nut; she will take
your hand and give you a road to the
horizon, to the place where Ra is. The doors
of the sky are open to you, the doors of the
firmament are thrown open to you, and
you will find Ra standing as he waits for
you; he will take your hand for you and
guide you to the two conclaves of the sky,
he will set you on the throne of Osiris.
(Mercer 2008, 207–208)

As the deceased king ascended through the cosmic
mother to his spiritual father, he was transformed into
an Akh. In Egyptian eschatology, the Akh was the
transfiguration of the dead to an eternal spirit. "Who were
transformed into something radiant through contact with
the sun-god and became a minor incarnation of the sun-god
themselves" (Kemp 2005, 159). After the transfiguration,
the king became "like Ra." Nut led the king to Ra, and Ra
sat him on the throne of Osiris. Throughout the Pyramid
Texts, the divine mother's words and actions transformed
the king as he ascended through the night sky. The king's
"Akh-making" occurred when the divine mother received
his spirit and birthed him into eternal life. He then traveled
the heavens to set in the west.

At night, the sun went on its journey through Nut's
body. The king, buried in the west, went through the same
cycle as the sun.

As a pure spirit, the king came into his transformation, rising like the solar deity Khepera. During his ascension, Ra embraced him. Now divine, the king became a god. Egyptian cosmology viewed the king as part of the cosmic order of stellar beings that rose and set like the sun.

The king came into spiritual being rising as Khepera on the horizon. Embraced by Atum, he became one with his father and lived forever as the son of the sun. In the funerary texts, each aspect of the solar god is instrumental in the ascension of the king. Utterance 222, which is titled "The king joins the sun god," describes the role of Khepera and Atum. The priest recited the following passages:

> Priest: Stand up upon this earth which originated from Ra, as the one who completes this spittle which came forth from Ra as the Bringer Into-Being. Come into being upon this earth, O royal vindicated one. Be exalted upon it, so that your Father, Ra may behold you. (Karenga 1984, 120)

> Priest: May you have power in your body, for you have no hindrance; you are born for Horus, you are conceived for Seth. Be pure in the Western Nome, receive your purification in the Heliopolitan Nome with your father, with Atum. Come into being, go up on high, and it will be well with you, it will be pleasant for you in the embrace of your father, in the embrace of Atum. O

Atum, raise this King up to you, enclose him within your embrace for he is your son of your body forever. (Faulkner, 50-51)

Photo by Author
Nut in an arched pose over the sky depicted in the Temple of Hathor, Dendera, Egypt.

# Nut: Tree Deity

Photo: Touregypt.net
Nut offering divine food and drink to the deceased at a sycamore
tree. The hieroglyphs on the tree spell Nut's name.
(The pot means "Nu" and the half loaf means "t.")

There were images of the tree of life in ancient Egyptian
temples associated with the divine mother. Trees were a

symbol of the maternal principle that life is given through nourishment. Both Nut and Hathor were associated with the sycamore tree (*Nehet*), which was a sacred tree in ancient Egypt. Nut and Hathor were both called "Lady of the Sycamore." The sycamore tree was sacred to both of them. (Kemp 2005, 53–54). Reliefs in various temples and tombs show Hathor as part of a sycamore tree. The sycamore tree was the national tree of ancient Egypt and was known as the southern sycamore. In the image above, Nut provides food and drink from the sycamore tree to the deceased, who are depicted in white garments. This image reflected the deceased who sought nourishment from the divine mother. She provided a mother's milk or water. As the divine mother, she nurtured the deceased and secured the king's transition to eternal life by feeding him water and milk as the natural mother did on earth. Divine mothers were frequently represented as suckling the kings, especially the ancient mother deities of southern and northern prehistoric kingdoms.

> The two vultures with long hair and hanging breasts; … they draw their breasts over the mouth of King Pepi, the two crowns of the two kingdoms personified as goddesses: The Pyramid text states, "This King Pepi knows his mother, he forgets not his mother; (even) the White Crown shining and broad that dwells in Nekheb, mistress of the southern palace.. and the bright Red Crown, mistress of the regions of Buto. O mother of this King Pepi …

give thy breast to this King Pepi, suckle this
King Pepi therewith." To this the divinity
responds: "O my son Pepi, my King, my
breast is extended to thee, that thou mayest
suck it, my King and live, my King as long
as thou art little." (Breasted 1959, 130)

In the tomb of King Pepi, Nut provided divine milk for
the king, which allowed him to live and wear the crown of
authority in the celestial realm.

The nourishing role of the divine mother was symbolized
as a tree in the Pyramid Texts and coffin texts, providing
the dead with the food and drink they needed to live in the
afterlife. Representing the divine mother, the sycamore tree's
image was included on the inside and outside of the coffins.
This tree was the national tree of ancient Egypt. Sycamore
trees fed the animals, birds, and humans. They provided
shade, homes, and were symbols of maternity. The sycamore
tree was prevalent in funerary imagery.

As a source of nourishment, the sycamore tree is an
appropriate emblem of the divine mother. The description
of the sycamore fig tree below describes its importance as
a source of nourishment for humans, animals, and birds in
Africa.

Photo: istock
A sycamore tree by a river.

The Sycamore Fig Tree (Ficus sycomorus), is a member of the family Moracea, which also includes the common edible fig. The species is found in various parts of Africa south of the Sahara Desert. Although it is sometimes found in woodland, these trees grow in riverine areas. The genus is ancient, being at least 60 million years old. The Sycamore Fig Tree can attain great heights, sometimes growing 15 meters or more. It is quite easy to identify, having a distinctive yellowish bark and fluted, buttressed trunk. The wood is soft, making it unsuitable for most purposes. In Uganda, the paper-like bark is used to make the very distinctive bark cloth, while in ancient Egypt the wood was used to fabricate coffins.

It produces an abundance of fruit all year round. The prolific crop is an important source of nourishment, being eaten by animal and bird species. Monkeys and baboons, birds and bats eat the fruit directly from the branches, while antelope and warthogs devour what falls to the ground.

The figs, although edible, are much smaller and harder than those which are domestically cultivated. They are the size of a marble and vary in color from yellow and brown to white. The fig is a false fruit, with hundreds of flowers being inside the almost closed, urn-shaped receptacle. (sabisabi.com)

Photo: istock
Sycamore figs.

In the Egyptian funerary text "The Book of Coming Forth by Day," there were two sycamore trees that stood at the eastern gate of heaven. Ra showed himself between the trees each morning. The dead were buried in coffins made of sycamore wood, returning their bodies to the womb of the divine mother. In chapter 59, the deceased, Osiris in the formula for breathing air and obtaining water in the necropolis, said, "O you Sycamore of Nut, give me the water and air in you!" (Lichtheim 2006, 122). The vignettes in this chapter and the reliefs in the private tombs show Nut emerging from the branches of a sycamore to pour water for the dead. The divine mother was responsible for insuring that what was needed to live in the afterlife was provided to the deceased. The dead needed the same resources to be reborn into an eternal life as they needed during their life on earth.

Photo: en.wikipedia.org
An image from the tomb of Thutmose III, depicting him drinking from the breast of the Tree (Isis) with her name in lower left as throne.

Already the Pyramid Texts suggest one
(Pyr. 916b {470}) and two sycamores (Pyr.
1433b {568}) in the eastern sky and the
Coffin Texts refer to two sycamores of
turquoise from within which Ra comes
forth (CT II, 367a-b {159}) Later we find
this motif in BD 96/97, 109 and 149. One
variant of the CT II 130h {203}) connects
the single sycamore as the resting place of
the deceased. (Billings, 39)

The Tomb of Qen-Amen shows him in
a partly destroyed scene sitting under a
magnificent sycamore with the goddess
standing in front of him. I am Nut, high
and great in the horizon. The deceased asks
his divine mother for provisions and water.
(Billings, 42)

Tree vignettes show an active goddess
providing the deceased with provisions. BD
124 (Billings, 43)

The sycamore was especially important in the royal
and funerary rituals and culture of ancient Egypt. When
someone died, a sycamore tree was often planted next to the
tomb. The sycamore was a symbol of the nourishment and
protection of Nut, as well as a symbol of the divine mother
herself. "Notably, the identification of several maternal
deities as tree goddesses also meant that burial in a wooden
coffin was viewed as a return to the womb of the mother as
tree goddess" (www.touregypt.net/tree goddesses). Images

of the divine mother as a tree goddess were found in the tomb of Sernedjein. In the tomb of Thutmose III, images of him suckling the breast of Isis in the form of a tree were found. King Ramese II, who ruled during the nineteenth dynasty, is depicted at the sacred sycamore tree (one of Het Heru's manifestations) in ceremony in the temple of Derr in occupied Nubia. (Higgins 2021, 71).

The sycamore fig exuded a white milky substance, which was why this tree was a symbol of a mother's milk. The imagery of the sycamore tree with the king in tombs and temples exemplified the maternal role of the tree as the nurturer. The mother goddess, through the image of the sycamore tree, provided the divine milk to the deceased king, which nourished him through the process of transforming him to an eternal spirit to reside with Ra.

# Conclusion

The Pyramid Texts written in the tombs of the Old Kingdom kings reflect the efforts of the priests to provide the king with a burial that contained the divine words to transition him to eternity. The fifth and sixth dynasties' tombs at Sakkara have been pieced together and stand as witness to the spiritual concepts concerning ancient Egyptian eschatology and the concept of eternal life. These ideas reflected ancient ideas told through an oral tradition and then inscribed on the walls of the tombs for eternity. From the writings in the tombs of the kings, and the imagery of Nut's body on the tomb ceilings, it is evident that she was instrumental in the rebirth and resurrection of the ka (spirit) in ancient Egypt's royal funerary rituals. Her role as the king's divine mother was maintained throughout Egyptian history. Nut transitioned the sun through the heavens (Duat) and birthed the sun every day. The birth of the sun was depicted as the birth of a child from a mother's watery womb. For the Egyptians, the watery sky, or cosmic ocean, was an appropriate image for the womb. The rebirth of the spirit required the same process as a natural birth. The burial in a coffin in the tomb (womb) was necessary to be spiritually reborn by the divine mother.

Nut, as the mother of Osiris, became the deceased king's spiritual mother upon his death and gave him life. The king travels through her (Duat) to his spiritual rebirth.

Just as the breast milk of the natural mother is required for the infant to grow, the newborn king required the milk of Nut to become divine and eternal. The Pyramid Texts tell us that the symbolism of the divine mother as a tree providing milk and sustenance to the deceased existed in the royal tombs of the king. The divine mother was expected to nourish the king as he transitioned to the afterlife by providing him with food and drink.

The drama of the sun's travels in the sky was depicted in the myths of the solar deity. Nut was imaged as the cosmic ocean in which the solar deity transited each day, and she provided a place for the king to live eternally. The ancient Egyptians expressed their ideas on immortality throughout their literature. Everywhere in their writings, you can find affirmation of immortality and eternal life. The conceptual separation of these components of the individual (i.e., the life force and the physical body) and the attribution of separate destinies is an indication of the level of insight the ancient Egyptians had concerning their perceived reality of death. They believed that after physical death, a spiritual rebirth was possible through the aid of the divine mother and other deities of the divine nine. The king, who represented humanity, could return to the heavens to become an imperishable star, and like the solar deity Ra, rise each morning on the eastern horizon. This daily rebirth and nightly return to the heavens (Duat) represented the spiritual cycle of renewal. The king returns to the womb of his heavenly mother for spiritual rebirth like his spiritual father Ra for eternity.

# Glossary

**Aker.** An earth god.

**Akh/Akhw.** The transfigured eternal spirit.

**Amen.** The god of Thebes, known as the "hidden one."

**Atum.** The creator god of Iunu.

**Book of Coming Forth by Day/Book of the Dead.** Scrolls of papyrus, or other objects, buried in Egyptian tombs with the deceased.

**Coffin Texts.** The text inscribed on the coffins of the deceased.

**Duat/netherworld.** The sky underneath the world.

**Ennead/divine nine.** The nine gods of Iunu headed by the creator god, Atum.

**Geb.** An earth god.

**Hathor.** A cow goddess and patroness of love and music.

**Horus.** The great sky god, and a symbol of kingship.

**Harkhety.** Horus of the horizon.

**Hu.** The deity personifying authoritative utterance.

**Isis/Aset.** The wife of Osiris and mother of Horus. The divine manifestation of the matrilineal authority.

**Iunu/Heliopolis.** The ancient city of the sun, and the place of the pillars from the Bible.

**ka.** The soul or spirit.

**Kamet.** Ancient Egypt.

**Khnum.** The creator of water and life.

**King Pepi.** A pharaoh of the Old Kingdom.

**King Teti.** A pharaoh of the Old Kingdom.

**Khepri/Khepera.** The personification of the rising morning sun.

**Mut.** The mother goddess.

**Ntr/Netcher.** To be godlike or divine.

**Nun.** The primordial water.

**Nut.** The sky goddess who is also referred to as the "sky," "heavens," and "divine mother."

**Old Kingdom.** A period in ancient Egypt (2650–2135 BCE).

**Pyramid Texts.** The oldest body of religious texts in ancient Egypt, discovered on the walls of chambers inside the pyramids of five kings of the fifth and sixth dynasties.

**Ra.** The sun god.

**Seth/ Setekh.** The brother of Osiris and Isis and rival of Horus.

**Shu.** The god of air.

**Tefnut.** The lion-headed goddess of moisture.

**Osiris/Wosir.** The god of the dead and son of Geb and Nut.

# References

Allen, James P. 2014. *Middle Egyptian: An Introduction to the Language and Culture of Hieroglyphs.* Cambridge: Cambridge University Press. Cambridge University Press.

Allen, James P. 1988. *Genesis in Ancient Egypt: The Philosophy of Ancient Egyptian Creation Accounts.* New Haven, CT:

Billings, Nils. *Writing an Image-The Formulation of the Tree Goddess Motif in the Book of the Dead.* 2004 Hamburg, Germany: Buske Verlag, Vol 32 p. 35-50.

Breasted, James Henry. 1959. *Development of Religion and Thought in Ancient Egypt.* New York: Harper & Row, Publishers.

Briffault, Robert. 1977. *The Mothers: A Study of the Origins of Sentiment and Initiations.* New Jersey: Humanities Press Inc.

Carruthers, Jacob H. 1995. *Mdw Ntr.* London: Karnak House.

Carruthers, Jacob H. 1992. *Essays in Ancient Egyptian Studies.* Los Angeles: University of Sankore Press.

Faulkner, Raymond. O. 2007. *The Ancient Egyptian Pyramid Texts.* Stilwell, KS: Digireads.com Publishing.

Faulkner, Raymond O. 2005. *Ancient Egyptian Book of the Dead.* New York: Fall River Press.

Gardner, Alan. 2012. *Egyptian Grammar*. Oxford: Griffith Institute Ashmolean Museum.

Higgins, Chester. 2021. *Sacred Nile*. Brooklyn, NY: March Forth Imprint.

Hornung, Erik, and Betsy M. Bryan, eds. 2002. *The Quest for Immortality Treasures of Ancient Egypt*. Washington D.C.: National Gallery of Art Publishers.

Karenga, Maulana. 1984. *The Husia: Sacred Wisdom of Ancient Egypt*. Los Angeles: The University of Sankore Press.

Kemp, Barry. 2005. *100 Hieroglyphs: Think Like an Egyptian*. London: Granta Books.

Lichtheim, Miriam. 2006. *Ancient Egyptian Literature Volume II: The New Kingdom*. Berkeley and Los Angeles California: University of California Press, LTD.

Lichtheim, Miriam. 1975. *Ancient Egyptian Literature Volume I: The Old and Middle Kingdoms*. Berkeley and Los Angeles: University of California Press, LTD.

Mercer, Samuel A. B. 2008. *The Pyramid Texts*. Forgotten Books. London, England United Kingdom.

Preston, James. 1982. *Mother Worship*. Chapel Hill, NC: University of North Carolina Press.

Wimby, Deidre. 1984. "The Female Horuses and Great Wives of Kamet Black Women in Antiquity." Edited by Ivan Van Sertima. Journal of African Civilizations Ltd., Inc.

https://egyptianmyths.net/tree.htm
https://www.sabisabi.com/wildfacts/sycamore-fig-tree/
http://sudhirahluwalia.com/biblical-plants/sacred-trees/
http://www.touregypt.net/featurestories/treegoddesses.htm

# About the Author

Safiya Karimah, M.A. Social Sciences, has been studying and researching ancient female deities for over twenty years. She has studied Egyptian literature, hieroglyphs, and history at various institutions. Her first publication was *Moon Goddess*, which explored the history of lunar worship and lunar goddesses. This book represents a continuation of the inquiry in the fields of history, astronomy, mother worship, religion, and ancient Egypt.

Printed in the United States
by Baker & Taylor Publisher Services